CLASSIC COCKTAILS

CLASSIC COCKTAILS

BEN REED

PHOTOGRAPHY BY WILLIAM LINGWOOD

RYLAND
PETERS
& SMALL

LONDON NEW YORK

Designers Saskia Janssen and Jo Fernandes
Senior Editor Miriam Hyslop
Production Manager Patricia Harrington
Art Director Anne-Marie Bulat
Publishing Director Alison Starling

Mixologist Ben Reed
Stylist Helen Trent

First published in the United Kingdom in 2006
by Ryland Peters & Small
20–21 Jockey's Fields
London WC1R 4BW
www.rylandpeters.com

10 9 8 7 6 5 4 3 2 1

Some of the recipes in this book were published in
Cool Cocktails and *The Cocktail Hour* by Ben Reed.

ISBN-10: 1-84597-226-0
ISBN-13: 978-1-84597-226-4

Printed in China.

CONTENTS

WHERE IT ALL BEGAN

The origin of the cocktail is steeped in colourful myth. The term 'cocktail' first appeared in an American dictionary in 1806 as a 'mixed drink of any spirit, bitters and sugar.'

Where the word cocktail first came from is anyone's guess. Some believe the cocktail was named after an Aztec princess called Xochitl. Others claim it was the innkeeper, Betsy Flanagan, who first coined the phrase. Betsy, they say, would tie chickens' tail feathers to mugs and cry 'Vive le Cock-tail!' to the French soldiers she was serving. Or does its origins lie in the French *coquetel* meaning mixed drink? Whatever its history, it wasn't until 1920s America that modern cocktail culture really took off.

Although many of the cocktails we now regard as 'classic' were invented before the 20th century, it was really the roaring twenties that saw cocktails come into their own. This happy time coincided with a most unhappy state of affairs in the USA – the social experiment called Prohibition (1920–1933). This era had a number of effects on drinking culture. It forced drinkers underground into illicit bars known as speakeasies. These bars weren't dives though – quite the opposite, they were luxurious and lavishly decorated and much more female friendly, which lent additional glamour to cocktails. Because alcohol was illegal, inferior bootleg spirit, or moonshine, was drunk, but was often so vile that bartenders would mix it with other juices and syrups to mask its aggressive flavour. The Long Island Iced Tea was created in these times, its seemingly innocuous name designed to fool the authorities. Drinks would also be served in mugs in an effort to distract the hapless police force.

Those American bartenders who didn't wish to break the law during Prohibition hotfooted it to Europe and Cuba to ply their trade anew in fresh surroundings, but with as much enthusiasm as ever. This was a particularly creative time for them. Many of the drinks we count as classics today, from the Bloody Mary to the daiquiri, were invented during this period, with the names of the bartenders who created them still hallowed in bars everywhere.

President Franklin D. Roosevelt had other ideas about Prohibition and it was repealed in 1933, shortly after he came to office. An accomplished drinker and handy bartender himself, F.D.R., along with Winston Churchill, was a great protagonist of, among other cocktails, the martini. Indeed, it was during a summit meeting between Joseph Stalin, Churchill and Roosevelt, in 1943, that Roosevelt first whipped up Dirty Martinis for his companions.

More should be said about the martini in this opening piece. The most iconic of cocktails, this drink has been enjoyed and tinkered with by a greater alumni of politicians, playwrights and playboys than has ever gathered around a bar. And it was these legendary drinkers who made cocktails the stuff of blurred anecdote and folklore, enshrined in times of glamour. Humphrey Bogart's dying words were reported to have been 'I should never have switched from Scotch to martinis' – perhaps not the most encouraging message for non-enthusiasts but a great quote none the less.

Women, never much welcome in bars, were welcomed with open arms to the cocktail lounges of the 1930s. Although there were still laws in some American states prohibiting women from ordering drinks at the bar, this was easily circumvented by implementing table service.

You may imagine that the 1940s bar was a place for reflection and austerity, mirroring the sombre post-war mood. Fortunately, a cocktail can be perfect for times of reflection as well as jubilation. The soldiers returning from the South Pacific to America told tales of the exotic Tiki cocktails made with rum and juices. Such tales prompted a cocktail menu trend that was championed by

bartending legend, Don the Beachcomber, (he was of such high repute that his status was of that usually afforded only to movie stars) and, to a lesser degree, his pupil, Trader Vic. Zombies, Mai Tais and Scorpions were all to become drinks that not only stood the test of time but also remind people of sun-kissed beaches and tropical holidays.

However, by the 1960s, cocktail consumption was going nowhere. Free love, drug culture and the perceived stuffiness of cocktail lounges meant that cocktails didn't really move forward. And so to the next decade…. Cocktails went the same way that most things went in the 1970s – take your pick from the Tequila Sunrise to the Piña Colada, the seventies did to the cocktail what, well, the seventies did to everything else.

The 1980s didn't help the situation at all, nor did the Thatcher and Reagan mentality. Spirits (and bank balances) were high, but never more so than when it came to the potency of cocktails. For some reason, bartenders seemed to do their damnedest to stifle the creativity of cocktail making by performing such demeaning feats as stuffing candy bars and jelly beans into bottles of vodka and selling them at dirt cheap prices.

Who knows what lies in store for the cocktail in the next millennium? One thing I guarantee, however, is that there is a cocktail for everyone and for every occasion; it's just down to you to experiment with some recipes and find the right one for you.

EQUIPMENT

For the aspiring home bartender, getting the right equipment can be as important as the taste of the final drink itself. You will probably find that you already have most of what you need to make cocktails in your own kitchen. But if you want to create the right atmosphere for your guests and mix cocktails with a little more flair, it's worth getting a few accessories.

MEASURE The measure is an essential piece of equipment for making cocktails. Measures come in a variety of sizes, from the single shot of 25 ml to 175 ml for a small glass of wine. If you can find the dual measure (one end holds 25 ml, the other 50 ml) you are starting off on the right foot. Your common or garden teaspoon will also be useful for measuring smaller quantities.

SHAKER The item most synonymous with the world of the 'spiritual advisor' is the cocktail shaker. While there are only two basic types of shaker – the three-piece (or deco) shaker and the modern-day professional bartender's (M.P.B.) favourite, the Boston shaker – they can come in many shapes and sizes from the rather apt fire extinguishers to the more abstract lighthouses and penguins. The three-piece (so named as it comes in three pieces – the can, the strainer and the lid) is suitable for home creations and for the more elegant world of the hotel bartender. Bartenders prefer the Boston shaker, purely for ergonomic reasons. Its two separate parts (the mixing glass and the can) allow the bartender more volume and yield greater results in the shake.

STRAINER Whenever possible, strain your concoction over fresh ice as the ice you have used in your shaker will already have started to dilute. If the Boston is your tool of choice, you will need something to strain the liquid out while keeping the ice in. There are two types of strainer – the Hawthorn strainer will sit happily over the metal part of the shaker, while the Julep fits comfortably in the mixing glass.

BARSPOON and MUDDLER The barspoon (or Bonzer) is the Swiss army knife of the cocktail world. This tool comes in a number of styles; the long, spiral stemmed, flat-ended spoon is the most versatile. As well as all the obvious uses for a spoon (measuring and stirring), the spiral stem and flat end is perfect for creating layered drinks (see page 17). The flat end can also be used for gentle muddling (dissolving powders into liquid, for example). If more labour intensive muddling is needed, you may want a more user-friendly piece of equipment. The muddler and the imaginatively titled 'wood' or 'stick' are more ergonomic and won't cause you as much discomfort as the Bonzer.

POURER Though not essential to the home bar, one of the tools that the M.P.B. finds indispensable is the pourer (a thin stainless steel spout mounted on a tapered plastic bung). This piece of equipment lets us pour a liquid at a regulated rate. M.P.B.s count to a fixed number when pouring a spirit or liqueur through a pourer, so a measure isn't necessary. Different spirits will pour at different speeds, however, depending on the amount of sugar in the liquids.

STRAWS For those of you starting off in the world of cocktails, a straw is an essential tool. In much the same way that a chef will always taste a sauce before serving it, you will need a method to hygienically test the balance of your drink. Dip a straw into the beverage in question and once submerged, place your finger over the top end to create a vacuum. Take the straw from the drink and suck the liquid from the straw — this small amount will be enough for you to determine whether your drink needs more sweetening or souring agent. This is called the pipette method and is used by bartenders all over the world when creating new drinks.

BLENDER Although the blender is an essential tool for any bar, I'm not a fan of blended drinks. I'll make them, sure, but I'd rather make something that isn't instantly turned to watery mush at the flick of a switch. And besides, it's very difficult to entertain your guests over the noise of a blender at full speed. A prosaic kitchen blender should suffice. Try to use crushed ice rather than cubes in the blender — it will add years to the life of its blades.

ICE Ice is another essential (and often overlooked) tool of every bartender. If you are making ice at home, make sure you use mineral rather than tap water to avoid having chlorinated ice cubes. There are three different types of ice: cubed, crushed and shaved. Cubed ice will melt (and therefore dilute) at a much slower rate but will also chill a cocktail less effectively than crushed or shaved ice. Drinks using crushed ice have risen in popularity recently, owing mostly to the arrival on the cocktail scene of concoctions like the Caipirinha and the Mojito. Shaved ice is mostly used in drinks that might require a little dilution to make them more palatable (remember, water is an important ingredient in a great many mixed drinks) and where they need to be absolutely as cold as possible.

GLASSWARE

Contrary to popular belief, you do not need to have an exhaustive range of glasses to create great cocktails. The glasses below should cover your needs.

The SHOT GLASS is fairly self-explanatory; it usually holds either a single or a double shot and is used for serving shots and shooters. It can also be used as a measure should you lose yours (a common occurrence even for the pros).

The OLD-FASHIONED GLASS (also known as the ROCKS GLASS or TUMBLER) is used for drinks that are served on the rocks (short drinks over ice). It should have a capacity of about 350 ml and can also house drinks like whisky and soda.

The HIGHBALL GLASS is a tall thin glass used for long cocktails and also for serving spirits with mixers. Anything over 350 ml should suffice.

HEATPROOF GLASS
For serving hot drinks, take your pick from the wine-glass-shaped Irish coffee glass to the type of tall glass in which you might be served a café latte in a smart restaurant.

You will need a WINE GLASS and a CHAMPAGNE FLUTE of some shape. As there is no real restriction on these, you can be as ornate as you choose.

A MARTINI GLASS is a must for any aspiring mixologist. The longer the stem, the more ornate. Martini glasses holding between 150 ml and 200 ml should suffice for drinks that are served straight up.

A MARGARITA COUPETTE is useful but not essential. This glass is also called the Marie Antoinette (so named as it is rumored the glass was shaped around the curve of her breast).

The HURRICANE GLASS is a multi-purpose glass, which comes in a number of different shapes and sizes. Generally seen as a glass that holds punches and frozen drinks, it is also known as the TULIP.

TECHNIQUES

There are six basic techniques behind the creation of a cocktail – layering, building, stirring, muddling, shaking and blending. When creating a mixed drink, it is important to remember two of the principles of cocktail making – first, to marry the flavours of the ingredients and secondly, to chill the ingredients. These simple principles can be applied to virtually any mixed drink. The only exception to this rule is the layered drink.

SHAKING (1) Drinks that contain heavy ingredients need an aggressive method of mixing and chilling. You will find that a good, sharp shake will bring life to 'heavy' ingredients. When shaking a cocktail there are a few things to remember. Whether you are using a three-piece shaker or a Boston, make sure you have one hand at each end of the shaker and shake vertically, making sure the ice and liquid travel the full distance of the shaker. When using a Boston, the cocktail should always be made in the mixing glass, so those who are enjoying the spectacle of your labour can see what is going into the drink (it's not that complex guys, honestly!). Add as much ice to the mixing glass as possible and attach the can squarely over the top to create a vacuum. Shake sharply until the outside of the stainless steel part of the shaker frosts over. When creating a shaken cocktail, always pour from the metal part of the shaker (it has a lip to stop the liquid dribbling down the outside of the vessel and the metal will help to sustain the temperature of the drink).

POUSSE CAFE or LAYERING (2) Literally meaning 'push coffee', the Pousse Café was invented by the French and was served as an accompaniment to coffee, the two being sipped alternately. To layer a cocktail, there are a couple of rules that need to be adhered to. First, choose spirits that will look dramatic when layered on top of one another in the glass. There isn't much point in layering liquids if they are of the same colour. Secondly, layer each liquid in order of density – this means adding the heaviest spirits first as they will sit at the bottom of the glass. The lower the alcohol content in a spirit and the greater the sugar level, the denser the liquid will be. Therefore, the spirit or liqueur that is the sweetest and has the lowest proof (percentage of alcohol) should be poured into the glass first. The higher the proof and the lower the sugar content, the lighter the spirit is. Be warned – this technique requires a steady hand. Pour your first ingredient into the shot glass. Pour your second down the spiral stem of a barspoon with the flat end resting on the surface of the liquid below.

BUILDING (3) Building is the term used to describe pouring a drink into a glass, one ingredient after another. It is the technique you would use to make a tall drink such as a gin and tonic or a Screwdriver. Once 'built' in the glass, the mixture may need a quick stir with a barspoon or the addition of a swizzle stick. When building a drink, always add as much ice to the glass as possible.

STIRRING (4) When the ingredients in a drink are all alcoholic, the best method of mixing and chilling them is stirring. Stirred drinks should always be made in the mixing glass. If you have the time, chill the glass first by adding ice and stirring gently with a barspoon (make sure any dilution is discarded before the alcohol is added), or place the glass in the freezer for an hour prior to making

the drink. When stirring a drink, place your spoon in the glass and gently stir the ice in a continuous manner. Add all the ingredients and continue stirring until the liquid is as cold as it can be (about 32°F). You may find it easier to strain the drink from the mixing glass using a Julep strainer.

MUDDLING (5) Muddling a drink may require the use of a barspoon, a muddler or a stick, depending on the intensity of the muddling. As opposed to stirring, a muddled drink will invariably incorporate the intentional dilution of ice at some stage. Whether releasing the flavour or aroma of a herb (such as mint in the Mojito), dissolving powder into a liquid (such as sugar into the Old-Fashioned), or extracting the juices of a fruit (such as fresh limes in a Caipirinha), the tool may change but the method is the same.

BLENDING You would usually be called upon to blend a drink when its ingredients involve heavy dairy products (as in the Piña Colada) or fresh fruit and frozen variations on classic drinks (strawberry daiquiris or frozen margaritas). Always use already-crushed ice in a blender and blend for about 20 seconds. When adding the crushed ice, the key phrase is 'less is more.' Add too much ice and the drink becomes solid in constitution (and then what do you have to do? That's right, add more liquid!). Add a little ice at a time though and you can achieve the perfect thickness. Blending a cocktail will invariably produce an ultra cold, thirst-quenching cocktail. Since the ice is crushed, the drink will dilute or separate quite quickly though. Be warned, no one likes a slushy cocktail!

FLAMING Although not strictly a method of cocktail creation, this is a flamboyant means of adding a little theatre to the cocktail occasion. A liquid has to be over 40 per cent alcohol to ignite and even then it's often difficult to get the flame to catch. A simple way to overcome this problem is to warm the glass with hot water first. However, with very high alcohol spirits this will not be necessary. Be careful though, these spirits can often react quite aggressively and on no occasion should you ever try to ignite them from the bottle!

GIN

Pink Gin is a thoroughly British cocktail that deserves
a premium gin. Although it originated as a medicinal potion
in the British Navy, Pink Gin became one of the most stylish
drinks in 1940s London.

pink GIN

50 ml gin
a dash of Angostura bitters

Rinse a frosted sherry
or martini glass with
Angostura bitters, add
chilled gin and serve.

smoky MARTINI

50 ml gin
a dash of dry vermouth
a dash of whisky

This is a variation on the FDR
Martini, with the whisky
substituting for the olive brine,
but the method is identical.

*The Classic Dry Martini has long been considered
the ultimate in sophistication and elegance.
Its roots date back as far as the 1840s, where
it is believed to have been served at a bar
in Martinez, California. The FDR (named after
President Roosevelt) and the smoky Martini
are popular variations on the stylish classic.*

fdr MARTINI

also known as the dirty martini
50 ml gin
a dash of dry vermouth
12.5 ml olive brine
green olive, to garnish

Add the gin, a dash of dry
vermouth and the olive brine to
a shaker filled with cracked ice.
Shake sharply and strain into a
frosted martini glass. Garnish
with an olive. Made to Mr.
Roosevelt's specifications!

classic dry
MARTINI

50 ml gin
a dash of dry vermouth
green olive, to garnish

Using a mixing glass, chill
the gin and vermouth over
ice and pour into a frosted
martini glass. Garnish with
a green olive.

The Bronx dates back to the days of Prohibition, when gang bosses reigned and booze played an important part in the economy of the underworld. Different areas of New York became known for the special cocktails they offered, such as this speciality of the Bronx. Like the Manhattan, it has three variations: the dry, the sweet and the perfect. The Silver and Golden Bronx are variations on the perfect, with the addition of egg white or egg yolk.

silver BRONX

50 ml gin
a dash of dry vermouth
a dash of sweet vermouth
50 ml fresh orange juice
1 egg white

Shake all the ingredients vigorously over ice and strain into a chilled cocktail glass.

golden BRONX

The method is the same as above, but substitute an egg yolk for the egg white.

The Journalist, another classic gin cocktail, is a good pre-dinner drink to order at a bar. If you are making a Journalist at home, watch the measurements carefully; it's a drink that needs to be very finely balanced. Made popular in the 1930s, the Gin Gimlet should be shaken vigorously to make sure the cocktail is chilled to perfection, then strained carefully before serving to catch any chips of ice.

the JOURNALIST

25 ml gin
a dash of sweet vermouth
a dash of dry vermouth
2 dashes of fresh lemon juice
2 dashes of triple sec
2 dashes of Angostura bitters

Shake all the ingredients over ice and strain into a frosted martini glass.

gin GIMLET

50 ml gin
25 ml lime cordial

Pour the gin and cordial
into a shaker filled with ice.
Shake very sharply and
pour through a strainer into
a frosted martini glass.

Two offshoots of the original Gin Fizz, (a classic that some would say should remain untouched), these cocktails have now become classics in their own right. The substitution of champagne for the soda water in the Royal Gin Fizz helps to make it special and lends it a little extra fizz (surely no harm there!). The addition of the rose flower water in the New Orleans or Ramos Fizz accentuates the juniper flavour in the gin and the dash of cream gives this very light drink a little more body.

royal
GIN FIZZ

50 ml gin
25 ml fresh lemon juice
1 barspoon white sugar
   (or 25 ml sugar syrup)
champagne, to top up
1 egg white

Put the egg white, gin, lemon juice and sugar into a shaker filled with ice and shake vigorously. Strain into a collins glass filled with ice. Top with champagne.

new orleans
FIZZ

also known as the ramos fizz

50 ml gin
25 ml fresh lemon juice
1 barspoon white sugar
   (or 25 ml sugar syrup)
25 ml rose flower water
   (or orange flower water)
25 ml single cream
a dash of egg white
soda water, to top up

Add all the ingredients, except the soda water, to a shaker filled with ice. Shake vigorously and strain into a highball glass over ice. Top with soda.

VODKA

The Black and White Russians are classics that have been on the scene since the Cold War era. They make stylish after-dinner cocktails with their sweet coffee flavour, which is sharpened up by the vodka. The White Russian, with its addition of the cream float, is even more appropriate as a nightcap.

black RUSSIAN

50 ml vodka
25 ml Kahlúa coffee liqueur
stemmed cherry, to garnish

Shake the vodka and Kahlúa together over ice and strain into a rocks glass filled with ice. Garnish with a stemmed cherry.

white RUSSIAN

For a White Russian, layer 25 ml light cream into the glass of a Black Russian over the back of a barspoon. Garnish with a stemmed cherry.

silver
STREAK

25 ml chilled vodka
25 ml kümmel

Pour a generous single measure
of chilled vodka into a rocks glass
filled with ice. Add a similar
amount of kümmel, stir gently
and serve.

A classic in its own right, the first Vodkatini dates back to the 1950s. As with the Classic Dry Martini, there are four important things to consider when it comes to making it: the quantity of vermouth, to shake or stir, straight up or on the rocks and finally, an olive or a twist. The Silver Streak features the liqueur kümmel and has a distinctive, aniseed-like taste that comes from the caraway seeds used in its production.

VODKATINI

50 ml vodka
a dash of dry vermouth
pitted olive or lemon zest, to garnish

Fill a mixing glass with ice and stir with a barspoon until the glass is chilled. Tip the water out and top with ice. Add a dash of dry vermouth and continue stirring. Strain the liquid away and top with ice. Add a large measure of vodka and stir in a continuous circular motion until the vodka is thoroughly chilled (taking care not to chip the ice and dilute the vodka). Strain into a frosted martini glass and garnish with either a pitted olive or a twist of lemon zest.

The story goes that Harvey, a California surfer who had performed particularly badly in an important contest, visited his local bar to drown his sorrows. He ordered his usual screwdriver – only to decide that it wasn't strong enough for what he had in mind. Scanning the bar for something to boost his drink, his eyes fell on the distinctively shaped Galliano bottle, a shot of which was then added to his drink as a float.

harvey
WALLBANGER

50 ml vodka
25 ml Galliano
fresh orange juice
orange slice, to garnish

Pour a large measure of vodka into a highball glass filled with ice. Fill the glass almost to the top with orange juice and pour in a float of Galliano. Garnish with an orange slice and serve with a swizzle stick and straw.

bloody MARY

50 ml vodka
200 ml tomato juice
2 grinds of black pepper
2 dashes of Worcestershire sauce
2 dashes of Tabasco sauce
2 dashes of fresh lemon juice
1 barspoon horseradish
1 celery stick, to garnish

Shake all the ingredients over ice
and strain into a highball glass
filled with ice. Garnish with a
celery stick. (These
measurements depend on
personal tastes for spices.)

The Bloody Mary has been a renowned hangover cure or pick-me-up for years. Curing hangovers can be painless and should be enjoyable, too. They are an aspect of bartending that cannot be ignored – and, in a truly biblical way, what the bartender giveth, so shall he take away. The creation of the Moscow Mule celebrates the godsend that is ginger beer. It lends the Mule its legendary kick and an easy spiciness.

moscow MULE

50 ml vodka
1 lime
ginger beer

Pour a large measure of
vodka into a highball filled
with ice. Cut the lime into
quarters, squeeze and drop
into the glass. Top with ginger
beer and stir with a
barspoon. Serve with a straw.

CITRUS martini

50 ml Cytryonowka vodka
25 ml lemon juice
25 ml Cointreau
a dash of sugar syrup
a lemon zest, to garnish

Add all the ingredients to a
shaker filled with ice, shake
sharply and strain into a
frosted martini glass. Garnish
with the lemon zest.

*Every martini should be made using the very
finest ingredients. Make this martini the 'ultimate'
by choosing from the exceptional quality spirits
now available. The Citrus Martini needs to be
shaken hard to take the edge off the lemon.
Try substituting lime for lemon for a slightly
more tart variation.*

ultimate MARTINI

a drop of Vya dry vermouth
50 ml well-chilled ultra-premium
  gin or vodka
twist of lemon or olive, to garnish

Rinse a frosted martini glass with
the vermouth. Add the gin (or
vodka) and garnish with a twist
of lemon or an olive.

This fresh fruit cooler always appeals due to the nature of the ingredients — there just seems to be something about raspberries in cocktails that everyone enjoys! Try the Vodka Collins for a sharp, zingy, thirst quencher on a hot day. Be warned, it's easy to forget there is alcohol in the drink!

raspberry RICKEY

4 fresh raspberries, plus 1 to garnish
50 ml vodka
20 ml fresh lime juice
a dash of Chambord
soda water, to top up

Muddle the raspberries in the bottom of a highball glass. Fill with ice, add the remaining ingredients and stir gently. Garnish with a fresh raspberry and serve with two straws.

vodka COLLINS

50 ml Vox vodka
20 ml fresh lemon juice
15 ml sugar syrup
soda water, to top up
lemon slice, to garnish

Build the ingredients into a highball glass filled with ice. Stir gently and garnish with a lemon slice. Serve with two straws.

dry MANHATTAN

50 ml rye whiskey
25 ml dry vermouth
a dash of Angostura bitters
lemon zest, to garnish

sweet MANHATTAN

50 ml rye whiskey
25 ml sweet vermouth
a dash of orange bitters
maraschino cherry, to garnish

For each of the variations, add the ingredients to a mixing glass filled with ice (make sure all ingredients are very cold) and stir the mixture until chilled. Strain into a frosted martini glass, add the garnish and serve.

WHISKY

The naming of Manhattan Island has an anecdotal history that links it with the cocktail. 'Manhachtanienck', which roughly translates as 'the island where we became intoxicated', was so named in the early 17th century by Lenape Indians after drinking a dark spirit.

perfect
MANHATTAN

50 ml rye whiskey
12.5 ml sweet vermouth
12.5 ml dry vermouth
a dash of Angostura bitters
orange zest, to garnish

old FASHIONED

50 ml bourbon
1 white sugar cube
2 dashes of orange bitters
orange zest, to garnish

Place the sugar cube soaked with orange bitters into a rocks glass, muddle the mixture with a barspoon and add a dash of bourbon and a couple of ice cubes. Keep adding ice and bourbon and keep muddling until the full 50 ml has been added to the glass (making sure the sugar has dissolved). Edge the glass with a strip of orange and drop it into the glass.

The Old Fashioned, the Rusty Nail and the Mint Julep have one thing in common – they are all timeless whisky cocktails that never fail to delight. As those among us who are already connoisseurs of the water of life will tell you, each cocktail should be serenaded with a few gentle words of seduction, sipped and, finally, savoured.

rusty NAIL

25 ml whisky
25 ml Drambuie
orange zest, to garnish

Add both ingredients to a glass filled with ice and muddle with a barspoon. Garnish with a zest of orange.

mint JULEP

50 ml bourbon
2 sugar cubes
5 sprigs of mint, to garnish

Crush the mint and sugar cubes in the bottom of a collins glass. Fill the glass with crushed ice and add the bourbon. Stir the mixture vigorously with a barspoon and serve.

The classic Sour is made with Scotch whisky, but since I like my sours a little on the sweet side, I prefer the vanilla sweetness of this bourbon-based Boston Sour. Reputed to be the very first cocktail, the Sazerac has been around since the 1830s. To enjoy its flavours fully, drink it undiluted.

boston SOUR

50 ml bourbon
25 ml fresh lemon juice
2 barspoons sugar syrup
2 dashes of Angostura bitters
a dash of egg white
lemon slice and
   maraschino cherry, to garnish

Add all the ingredients to a shaker filled with ice and shake sharply. Strain the contents into an old-fashioned glass filled with ice; garnish with a lemon slice and a maraschino cherry.

new orleans
SAZERAC

50 ml bourbon
25 ml Pernod
1 sugar cube
a dash of Angostura bitters

Rinse an old-fashioned glass with Pernod
and discard the Pernod. Put the sugar in
the glass, saturate with Angostura bitters,
then add ice cubes and the bourbon
and serve.

The Hot Toddy, with its warming blend of spices and sweet honey aroma, has long been the perfect comforter and will soothe any aches, snuffles and alcohol withdrawal symptoms that your illness may have inflicted upon you. It's also a great life-saver for cold afternoons spent outside watching sport. Next time you need to pack a thermos flask of coffee, think again – mix up a batch of Hot Toddies and see how much more popular you are than the next spectator!

hot TODDY

50 ml whisky
25 ml fresh lemon juice
2 barspoons honey or sugar syrup
75 ml hot water
1 cinnamon stick
5 whole cloves
2 lemon slices

Spear the cloves into the lemon slices and add them to a heatproof glass or a toddy glass along with the rest of the ingredients.

RUM & CACHAÇA

The Mai Tai was originally made in the 1940s by Victor Bergeron (Trader Vic) in California. With its complex mixture of flavours it has as many variations as it has garnishes. The one thing that most bartenders seem to agree on is that a thick, dark rum should be used, along with all the fruit-based ingredients that lend the classic its legendary fruitiness.

MAI TAI

50 ml Demerara rum
15 ml orange curaçao
15 ml apricot brandy
20 ml fresh lemon or lime juice
a dash of Angostura bitters
2 dashes of orgeat syrup
50 ml fresh pineapple juice
a mint sprig, to garnish

Add all the ingredients to a cocktail shaker filled with ice, shake and strain into an ice-filled old-fashioned glass. Garnish with a mint sprig. Serve with straws.

The Original Daiquiri is a classic cocktail that was made famous in the El Floridita restaurant in Havana early in the 20th century. It has as many recipe variations as it has famous drinkers (Hemingway always ordered doubles at El Floridita), but once you have found the perfect balance, stick to those measurements exactly. The Orange Daiquiri and Bacardi Cocktail are two of the best-known variations.

bacardi
COCKTAIL

50 ml Bacardi white rum
a dash of grenadine
juice of 1 small lime
1 barspoon of castor sugar
or a dash of sugar syrup

Shake all the ingredients
sharply over ice, then strain
into a frosted martini glass
and serve.

orange
DAIQUIRI

50 ml Creole Schrubb rum
25 ml fresh lemon juice
2 barspoons sugar syrup

Measure all the ingredients and
pour into an ice-filled shaker.
Shake and strain into a frosted
martini glass.

original
DAIQUIRI

50 ml golden rum
25 ml fresh lime juice
3 barspoons sugar syrup

Measure all the ingredients
and pour into an ice-filled
shaker. Shake and strain into
a frosted martini glass.

A sweet, creamy drink that, for a time, epitomized the kind of cocktail disapproved of by 'real' cocktail drinkers (compare a Piña Colada with a Classic Dry Martini). However, since its creation in the 1970s, it has won widespread popularity, and, now that we are in the new millennium, cocktails are for everyone, so there's no shame in ordering this modern-day classic at the bar.

piña
COLADA

50 ml golden rum
25 ml coconut cream
12.5 ml cream
12.5 ml fresh pineapple juice
a slice of pineapple, to garnish

Put all the ingredients into a blender, add a scoop of crushed ice and blend. Pour into a sour or collins glass and garnish with a slice of pineapple.

The Rum Runner is a perfect example of rum's affinity with fresh juices. Rum also has the ability to hold its own when combined with quite a selection of other flavours. The Planter's Punch is a great favourite for parties because it can be made in advance – prepared in an old oak barrel for authenticity, but a big bowl will do, with slices of fruit added. The T-Punch is a refreshing drink, perfect for a hot summer day and can be made according to taste with more lime or more sugar for a quick variation.

rum RUNNER

25 ml white rum
25 ml dark rum
juice of 1 lime
a dash of sugar syrup
150 ml fresh pineapple juice

Shake all the ingredients sharply over ice in a shaker and strain into a highball glass filled with crushed ice.

planter's PUNCH

50 ml Myers rum
juice of half a lemon
50 ml fresh orange juice
a dash of sugar syrup
soda water, to top up
orange slice, to garnish

Pour all the ingredients, except
the soda water, into a cocktail
shaker filled with ice, shake and
strain into an ice-filled highball
glass. Top up with soda water and
garnish with a slice of orange.

T-PUNCH

50 ml white rum
1 lime
1 brown sugar cube
soda water, to top up

Place the sugar cube in the
bottom of an old-fashioned glass.
Cut the lime into eighths,
squeeze and drop into the glass.
Crush gently with a pestle to
break up the sugar. Add the rum
and ice, then top up with soda.
Stir and serve.

The Mojito, with its alluring mix of mint and rum, invariably whisks its drinker away to warmer climes. Championed by Hemmingway in the 1940s and wildly popular in Miami for years, this Cuban concoction can now be found gracing the menus of discerning cocktail bars around the world.

MOJITO

50 ml golden rum
5 sprigs of mint
2 dashes of sugar syrup
a dash of fresh lime juice
soda water, to top up

Put the mint into a highball glass, add the rum, lime juice and sugar syrup, and crush with a barspoon until the aroma of the mint is released. Add the crushed ice and stir vigorously until the mixture and the mint are spread evenly. Top with soda water and stir again. Serve with straws.

One of the most famous of all rum-based drinks, the Cuba Libre was reputed to have been invented by an army officer in Cuba shortly after Coca-Cola was first produced in the 1890s. Cachaça, a spirit indigenous to Brazil, is distilled directly from the juice of sugar cane, unlike white rum, which is usually distilled from molasses. The Caipirinha has made cachaça popular in many countries.

CAIPIRINHA

50 ml cachaça
1 lime
2 brown sugar cubes

Cut the lime into eighths, squeeze and place in an old-fashioned glass with the sugar cubes, then crush well with a pestle. Fill the glass with crushed ice and add the cachaça. Stir vigorously and serve with two straws.

CUBA LIBRE

50 ml white rum
1 lime
cola

Pour the rum into a highball glass filled with ice; cut a lime into eighths, squeeze and drop the wedges into the glass. Top with cola and serve with straws.

TEQUILA

The Tequila Slammer is a drink that needs to be handled with care. This one is more likely to be imbibed for the sensation rather than the taste!

tequila SLAMMER

50 ml gold tequila
50 ml champagne (chilled)

Pour both the tequila and the chilled champagne into a highball glass with a sturdy base. Hold a napkin over the glass (sealing the liquid inside), sharply slam the glass down on a stable surface and drink in one go while it's fizzing.

All you need to create a margarita is good-quality tequila, lime and orange-flavoured liqueur. Yet within the boundaries of these ingredients you can make your drink taste quite different. The type of tequila, the choice of sour, the brand of sweetener and the ratio of all three influence the final flavour. There is no such thing as the perfect margarita and the only person who can judge the levels of perfection is its recipient. Here are some simple recipes to get you started on the road of experimentation.

classic
MARGARITA

standard
50 ml gold tequila
20 ml triple sec
25 ml fresh lime juice
lime wheel, to garnish
salt (for the glass)

simple
50 ml tequila
20 ml orange juice
25 ml fresh lime juice
lime wheel, to garnish
salt (for the glass)

sames
25 ml gold tequila
25 ml Cointreau
25 ml fresh lime juice
lime wheel, to garnish
salt (for the glass)

strong
50 ml tequila
25 ml Grand Marnier
25 ml fresh lime juice
lime wheel, to garnish
salt (for the glass)

Add all the ingredients to a shaker filled with ice. Shake sharply and strain into a salt-rimmed, chilled margarita glass. Garnish with a lime wheel.
OR
For frozen margaritas, add all the ingredients to a blender, add one scoop of crushed ice and blend for 20 seconds. Pour into a margarita coupette and garnish with a lime wheel.

triple gold
MARGARITA

50 ml gold tequila
2 teaspoons Cointreau
2 teaspoons Grand Marnier
20 ml fresh lime juice
20 ml Goldschlager

Add all the ingredients except
the Goldschlager to a shaker filled
with ice. Shake sharply and strain
into a chilled margarita glass.
Float the Goldschlager onto the
surface of the mixture and serve.

Patrón rightfully stands up as a tequila to be counted. But be warned, its decanter-type bottle may have upped the price on this expensive tequila. Mixed with Citronage (a premium orange liqueur), this margarita is the drink you'd choose if money were no object. Layered with a float of Goldschlager, the Triple Gold Margarita will bring a touch of splendour to any bar menu. Laced with real 24 carat gold pieces, Goldschlager is a cinnamon-flavoured liqueur that adds considerably to the depth of taste of the cocktail.

la margarita
DE LE PATRON

50 ml Patrón Añejo tequila
30 ml Citronage
20 ml fresh lime juice
salt (for the glass)

Add all the ingredients
to a shaker filled with ice.
Shake sharply and strain
into a salt-rimmed, chilled
margarita coupette.

The prickly pear has become de rigueur *in cocktails and makes a great addition to the margarita. The average pear doesn't always contain enough flavour to carry the drink off so it's well worth spending that bit of extra time looking for prickly pears. Anything from strawberries to cranberries, blueberries to raspberries can be used in this recipe. Choose your own combination of seasonal berries for subtle variations.*

prickly pear
MARGARITA

50 ml silver tequila
20 ml triple sec
20 ml lime juice
a dash of grenadine
25 ml prickly pear purée
thin slice of pear, to garnish

Add all the ingredients to a shaker filled with ice. Shake sharply and strain into a chilled margarita glass. Garnish with a sliver of pear.

berry
MARGARITA

50 ml gold tequila
20 ml triple sec
20 ml fresh lime juice
a dash of crème de mure
seasonal berries of your choice,
    plus extra to garnish

Add all the ingredients to a
blender. Add two scoops of
crushed ice and blend for 20
seconds. Pour into a margarita
coupette and garnish with a berry.

BRANDY, LIQUEURS & APERITIFS

The Brandy Alexander is the perfect after-dinner cocktail, luscious and seductive and great for chocolate lovers. It's important, though, to get the proportions right so that the brandy stands out as the major investor.

BRANDY alexander

50 ml brandy
12.5 ml crème de cacao
   (dark and white)
12.5 ml double cream
nutmeg, to garnish

Shake all the ingredients over ice and strain into a frosted martini glass. Garnish with a sprinkle of nutmeg.

The Stinger is a great palate cleanser and digestif and, like brandy, should be consumed after dinner. The amount of crème de menthe added depends on personal taste.

The Sidecar, like many of the classic cocktails created in the 1920s, is attributed to the inventive genius of Harry MacElhone, who founded Harry's New York Bar in Paris. It is said to have been created in honour of an eccentric military man who would roll up outside the bar in the sidecar of his chauffeur-driven motorcycle. It is certainly the cocktail choice of people who know precisely what they want.

STINGER

50 ml brandy
25 ml crème de menthe (white)

Shake the ingredients together over ice and strain into a frosted martini glass.

SIDECAR

50 ml brandy
juice of half a lemon
12.5 ml Cointreau

Shake all the ingredients
together over ice and strain
into a frosted martini glass
with a sugared rim.

AMERICANO

25 ml Campari
25 ml sweet vermouth
soda water
1 orange slice, to garnish

Build the ingredients over ice
into a highball glass, stir and
serve with an orange slice.

The Americano and the Negroni have, of course, been around for a long time. The Americano is a refreshing blend of bitter and sweet, topped with soda water to make the perfect thirst quencher for a hot summer afternoon. The Negroni packs a powerful punch, but still makes an elegant aperitif. For a drier variation, add a little more dry gin, but if a fruity cocktail is more to your taste, wipe some orange zest around the top of the glass and add some to the drink.

NEGRONI

25 ml Campari
25 ml sweet vermouth
25 ml gin
orange zest, to garnish

Build all the ingredients into a rocks glass filled with ice, garnish with a twist of orange zest and stir well. For an extra-dry Negroni, add a little more gin.

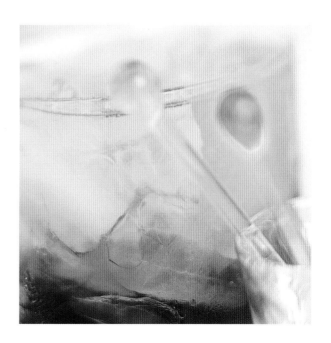

The Golden Cadillac is not a drink to be approached lightly and you could be excused for raising your eyebrows at the possibility of mixing crème de cacao (chocolate-flavoured liqueur) with orange juice and Galliano (herb and liquorice-flavoured). If the thought of this combination is too much for you, try substituting the crème de cacao with Cointreau to create another popular cocktail called Golden Dream. The Grasshopper is a more obvious combination of peppermint and cream, the perfect drink for after dinner.

golden CADILLAC

25 ml crème de cacao (white)
25 ml single cream
50 ml fresh orange juice
a dash of Galliano

Shake all the ingredients over ice, strain into a martini glass and serve.

GRASSHOPPER

25 ml crème de menthe (white)
12.5 ml crème de menthe (green)
12.5 ml single cream

Shake all the ingredients over ice, strain into a chilled martini glass and serve.

CHAMPAGNE

The Champagne Cocktail has truly stood the test of time, as popular now as when it was sipped by the stars of the silver screen in the 1940s. It's a simple and delicious cocktail that epitomizes the elegance and sophistication of that era and still lends that same touch of urbanity to those who drink it today.

champagne
COCKTAIL

25 ml brandy
1 white sugar cube
2 dashes of Angostura bitters
dry champagne

Moisten the sugar cube with Angostura bitters and place in a champagne flute. Add the brandy, then gently pour in the champagne and serve.

The Bellini originated in Harry's Bar in Venice in the early 1940s and became a favourite of the movers and shakers of chic society. Although there are many variations on this recipe, there is one golden rule for the perfect Bellini – always use fresh, ripe peaches to make the peach juice. If there is another drink in the world that looks more tempting and drinkable than a Black Velvet, then please, someone make it for me now. Pour this drink gently into the glass to allow for the somewhat unpredictable nature of both the Guinness and the champagne.

BELLINI

¼ fresh peach, skinned
12.5 ml crème de pêche
a dash of peach
   bitters (optional)
champagne, to top up
peach ball

Blend the peach and add to a champagne flute. Pour in the crème de pêche and the peach bitters, if using, and gently top up with champagne, stirring carefully and continuously. Garnish with a peach ball in the bottom of the glass, then serve.

BLACK VELVET

Guinness
champagne

Half-fill a champagne flute with
Guinness, gently top with
champagne and serve.

FRENCH 75

50 ml gin
25 ml fresh lemon juice
12.5 ml sugar syrup
champagne, to top up
lemon zest, to garnish

Shake the gin, lemon juice and
sugar syrup over ice and
strain into a champagne flute.
Top with champagne and
garnish with a long strip of
lemon zest.

The James Bond is a variation on the Champagne Cocktail, using vodka instead of the more traditional brandy. The naming of this cocktail is a mystery to me since the eponymous spy liked his drinks shaken! The French 75 is another classic cocktail from Harry's New York Bar in Paris. It's not dissimilar to a Gin Sling, but is topped up with champagne instead of soda water.

JAMES BOND

25 ml vodka
1 white sugar cube
2 dashes of Angostura bitters
champagne, to top up

Moisten the sugar cube with Angostura bitters and put it into a martini glass. Cover the sugar cube with the vodka and top with champagne.

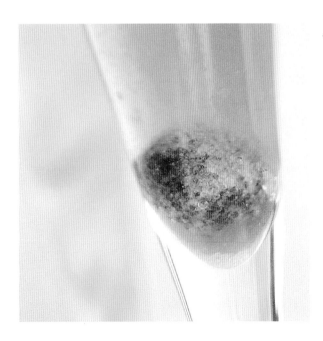

MIMOSA

½ glass champagne
fresh orange juice, to top up

Pour the orange juice over
half a flute-full of champagne
and stir gently.

It is thought that Alfred Hitchcock invented the Mimosa in an
old San Francisco eatery called Jack's sometime in the 1940s,
for a group of friends suffering from hangovers. The fruity
melody of flavours in the classic Apricot Royale combines with
the champagne to make this drink the perfect cure for the
blues. The Ginger Champagne is delicate yet different enough
to appease even the most sophisticated cocktail drinker.

apricot
ROYALE

50 ml apricot brandy
20 ml fresh lemon juice
20 ml sugar syrup
a dash of peach bitters
a dash of orange bitters
champagne, to float
apricot slice, to garnish

Add all the ingredients, except the
champagne, to a shaker filled with ice,
shake sharply and strain into a rocks
glass filled with ice. Gently layer a
float of champagne over the surface
of the drink. Garnish with an apricot
slice and serve.

ginger
CHAMPAGNE

2 thin fresh ginger slices
25 ml vodka
champagne, to top up

Put the ginger in a shaker and
press with a barspoon or
muddler to release the flavour.
Add ice and the vodka, shake and
strain into a champagne flute. Top
with champagne and serve.

NON-ALCOHOLIC

This one works both as a meal and a drink! To make it alcoholic, add a large measure of Baileys, which adds a kick and makes the drink even more viscous.

virgin banana
COLADA

1 ripe banana (reserve 1 slice, to garnish)
25 ml coconut cream
2 teaspoons double cream
150 ml pineapple juice

Add all the ingredients to a blender along with a scoop of crushed ice, and blend for 20 seconds. Pour into a hurricane glass and garnish with a banana slice. Serve with two straws.

There's nothing in the manual that says cocktails with no alcohol in them should be low maintenance. The Virgin Mary is a way of saying thank you to anyone who has taken on the noble role of designated driver for the night. Since this variation is without vodka, I tend to go a bit crazy on the spices to compensate! The Shirley Temple is a thirst quencher for the very sweet-toothed and, most appropriately, named after the famous Hollywood child actress.

VIRGIN MARY

300 ml tomato juice
2 grinds of black pepper
2 dashes of Tabasco sauce
2 dashes of Worcestershire
    sauce
2 dashes of fresh lemon juice
1 barspoon horseradish sauce
celery stalk, to garnish

Shake all the ingredients over ice and strain into a highball glass filled with ice. Garnish with a celery stalk.

shirley TEMPLE

25 ml grenadine
ginger ale or lemonade,
    to top up
lemon slice, to garnish

Pour the grenadine into a highball glass filled with ice and top with either ginger ale or lemon soda. Garnish with a slice of lemon and serve.

It's so simple, I defy anyone not to admit that a Cranberry Cooler, when served ice cold and in the right proportions, is the only thing that almost beats a lemonade made just right! The St. Clement's takes its name from the English nursery rhyme 'Oranges and Lemons said the bells of St. Clement's'.

CRANBERRY COOLER

soda water
cranberry juice
1 lime

Fill a tall highball glass with crushed ice. Pour in equal parts of soda water and then cranberry juice. Garnish with a squeeze of lime and serve with two straws.

ST. CLEMENT'S

bitter lemon
fresh orange juice
lemon slice, to garnish

Build both ingredients (the bitter lemon first) in equal parts into a highball glass filled with ice. Stir gently, garnish with a lemon slice, and serve with two straws.

Try using freshly squeezed pineapple juice instead of grapefruit in your Pussy Foot for a slightly sweeter variation. There's nothing quite like old school lemonade. On a hot day, experiment with soda water instead of water for that extra zing.

PUSSY FOOT

150 ml fresh orange juice
150 ml fresh grapefruit juice
a dash of grenadine
2 dashes of fresh lemon juice

Shake the ingredients well with ice and strain into a highball glass filled with ice.

old-fashioned LEMONADE

25 ml fresh lemon juice
50 ml sugar syrup
150 ml water
lemon wedge, to garnish

Add all the ingredients to a shaker filled with ice, shake sharply, then strain into a highball glass filled with ice. Garnish with a lemon wedge and serve.

INDEX

CONVERSION CHART

Measures have been rounded up or down slightly
to make measuring easier.

Imperial	Metric
½ oz.	12.5 ml
1 oz. (single shot)	25 ml
2 oz. (double shot)	50 ml
3 oz.	75 ml
4 oz.	100 ml
5 oz.	125 ml
6 oz.	150 ml
7 oz.	175 ml
8 oz.	200 ml